SOUTHEAST ALASKA

THE PANHANDLE

A Photo Memory

Photographed by Mark Kelley

Published by

Todd Communications

Published by Todd Communications
203 W. 15th Ave., Suite 102
Anchorage, Alaska 99501-5128
Phone: (907) 274-8633
Fax: (907) 276-6858
e-mail: info@toddcom.com

Printed in Korea by Samhwa Printing Co., Ltd.

20, 19, 18, 17, 16, 15, 14, 13, 12, 11, 10, 9, 8, 7, 6

Library of Congress Number 99-67499

Pages 2-3

Auke Village Recreation Area north of Juneau is named for the Auke tribe of Tlingit Indians. The original inhabitants of the Juneau area sited their village here. When summer-blooming fireweed goes to seed, locals know that snow will soon follow.

SOUTHEAST ALASKA

THE PANHANDLE

A Photo Memory

Photographed by Mark Kelley

Ketchikan Area

Right - Once housing bawdy houses and speakeasies, the buildings on Ketchikan's Creek Street stand on pilings. Wooden boardwalks serve as sidewalks. A red cable railway car carries visitors to the Cape Fox Lodge and Creek Street.

Below - A cruise ship docks at the wharf in Ketchikan, Alaska's southernmost city and the first stop for cruise and ferry passengers coming from the south. Ketchikan's airport is located on Gravina Island (background) and can be reached only by a ferryboat.

Next page - A sunset colors the waters of Tongass Narrows near Ketchikan. Located on Revillagigedo Island, this community of just under 14,000 is a hub of fishing and logging activity and the regional center for many towns and villages in the southern Panhandle.

Left -The Clan House and 14 poles at the Totem Bight State Park ten miles north of Ketchikan were carved in the late 1930s by artists employed by the Civilian Conservation Corps. Recreated by elder Tlingit carvers, the poles were modeled after the decaying totem poles salvaged from abandoned Tlingit and Haida villages in the area. The carving tools were handmade in the tradition that existed before Europeans explored and settled Southeast Alaska.

Right - A rain meter on the downtown dock records Ketchikan's legendary precipitation. The average yearly rainfall is 162 inches per year. Anchorage's average is 15.91 inches per year. Los Angeles, California's average is 14.77 inches per year.

Above - A carved eagle perches atop a pole at Ketchikan's Saxman Totem Park. The eagle and the raven represent the two clans of Tlingit and Haida society. Each person is either a raven or an eagle, depending on whether their mother is a raven or an eagle. Traditionally, a person married a member of the other group.

Next page - The state ferry M/V Columbia rounds Pennock Island as it departs Ketchikan. Most of the communities in Southeast Alaska are inaccessible by road and are linked by the ferries of the Alaska Marine Highway System. The Columbia carries up to 970 passengers and 180 vehicles and was built in 1974 at a cost of $22 million. Alaska state ferries are named for the state's glaciers.

7

Left - A raven tops a house post at the Saxman Totem Park. The raven is a clever and mischievous character who figures prominently in Tlingit, Haida and Tsimshian oral traditions as the creator of the world who brought daylight to a world of darkness. The common raven is a year-round resident throughout most of Alaska, the largest all-black bird in the world.

Below - Saxman Totem Park, located three miles south of Ketchikan, contains 24 poles, one of the largest collections in the world. Saxman is a Tlingit Indian village founded in 1894 when Indians in nearby villages resettled to have their own school and church and to be near work opportunities in Ketchikan.

Right - The Cape Fox Lodge overlooks Ketchikan's Creek Street. A rail car carries passengers up to the hotel and nearby civic center. The lodge was built by the Cape Fox Corporation, owned by Ketchikan area Indians.

Below - Floatplanes park at a dock in the Tongass Narrows at Ketchikan. Floatplanes fly mail, freight, passengers and visitors between Ketchikan and the water-bound towns and villages of Prince of Wales and Annette Islands.

Misty Fjords

Right - A floatplane flies over the entrance to Rudyerd Bay in Misty Fjords National Monument. The dramatic cliff of Punchbowl Cove rises 3,000 feet in the distance. The 2.2 million-acre wilderness, accessible only by boat or plane, was created by a law signed by President Jimmy Carter in 1978.

Below - Like other waterways of Misty Fjords National Monument, the vertical rock walls of Rudyerd Bay were carved by glaciers in the last ice age. Nex'adi Indians occupied this bay. Many Tlingit Indians in the Ketchikan area trace their ancestors to this area.

Next page - The steep walls of Punchbowl Lake dwarf a floatplane. The dramatic topography was created by a lava flow which plugged up a valley one-half million years ago.

Prince of Wales Island

Right - *A sea otter (Enhydra lutris) feeds while floating on its back. Sea otters eat sea urchins, crabs, clams, mussels, octopus and fish. An otter places the food on its chest eating it piece by piece, sometimes using a rock to crack shells. Thick pelts protect sea otters from cold water temperatures. The sea otter was nearly hunted to extinction by Russians in the 18th and 19th centuries.*

Below - *The fishing town of Craig was founded in 1911 when Canadian-born William Craig Millar built a salmon packing plant, saltery and cold storage plant there. Craig is the largest community on Prince of Wales Island, about 60 air miles west of Ketchikan. Logging, sport fishing and whale watching provide employment.*

Twenty-one totem poles, some original and some replicated, stand at the center of the Tlingit Indian village of Klawock on Prince of Wales Island. They are memorial and mortuary poles gathered mainly from the nearby abandoned winter village of Tuxekan.

Left - The rays of a wooden sun radiate from a pole in the Klawock Totem Park on Prince of Wales Island. Klawock began as a summer fishing camp for the Tahn-da-quan Indians of Moira Sound and was incorporated as a city in 1929.

Below - A full moon sets over Bucareli Bay just outside of Craig on Prince of Wales Island. It is the largest island in Southeast Alaska, measuring 135 miles long and 45 miles wide. The island's towns and logging camps are accessible to Ketchikan only by ferry and air service.

Left - *The bear at the top of a totem pole on Chief Shakes Island in Wrangell harbor commemorates how a grizzly bear led Tlingit Indians to safety on a nearby mountain peak to escape a great flood.*

Below - *Chief Shakes tribal house was reconstructed by the Civilian Conservation Corps in the late 1930s and is listed as a historic site on the National Register. The house and reconstructed totem poles are located on Chief Shakes Island in Wrangell's boat harbor. The building replicates the architecture of the communal long houses used by Tlingits before missionaries discouraged their use.*

Right - Petroglyphs, stone carvings, adorn the rocks above the high tide line near Wrangell. The oldest drawings were ground or pecked into the rocks by a maritime people who migrated to the area 10,000 years ago. More recent petroglyphs depict animals, fish or supernatural beings and were probably created by ancestors of the modern Tlingit Indians.

Below - Wrangell is strategically located on Wrangell Island, south of the broad mouth of the Stikine River which reaches 330 miles into Canadian British Columbia. It is the only Alaskan city to have existed under four nations and three flags: the Stikine Tlingit Indians, the Russians, Great Britain and the United States. The Stikine tribe of the Tlingit Indians lived nearby and used the Stikine River to trade with the Athabaskan Indians in modern-day Canada. The Russian-American Company established Fort Saint Dionysius in 1834 to solidify their fur otter trade with the Stikines. The British Hudson's Bay Co. leased it in 1839 and renamed it Fort Stikine. Under the Americans, who called it Fort Wrangell after the United States bought Alaska from the Russians in 1867, the town became an important supply point and staging center for Canadian gold rushes in 1861, 1873 and 1898.

Left - The wooden homes and warehouses along Hammer Slough in Petersburg are built on pilings to keep them high and dry during the rise and fall of the ocean tide.

Below - Commercial fishing boats line the waterfront of Petersburg. The town sits on Mitkof Island in view of the majestic Coast Mountains and is home to one of the state's most prosperous fishing fleets. Tlingit Indians inhabited the area long before Norwegian Peter Buschmann built a sawmill and fish cannery there in the late 1800s. Many of Petersburg's 3,400 residents trace their heritage to Norwegian immigrants.

Petersburg

Far Left - *Norwegian folk painting called rosemaling decorates the shutters of the Sons of Norway Hall and many storefronts in Petersburg.*

left - *A Viking ship replica, the Valhalla, is one of many features in the annual Little Norway Festival which Petersburg hosts every spring to celebrate Norwegian Independence Day. The event also includes Norwegian dance and music, a seafood feast, a parade and pageant.*

Below - *The Sons of Norway Hall was built on pilings over the Petersburg harbor in 1912 by the fraternal organization and is the center of social life in Petersburg.*

Left - Totem poles line the two-mile walk in the Sitka National Historical Park. The poles are copies of totems brought to Sitka by Alaska's Governor John Brady in 1905, retrieved from the Louisiana Purchase Exhibition in St. Louis the year before. The park is the site of the Battle of Sitka in 1804 between the Russian-American Company and the Kiksadi tribe of Tlingit Indians. It was the last major conflict between Europeans and Natives of the Northwest Coast.

Above - St. Michael's Russian Orthodox Cathedral dominates downtown Sitka, in the middle of the town's main street. Built in the 1840s, the original structure burned in 1966, but residents were able to save most of the church's prized icons (sacred paintings decorated with gold and jewels) and historic furnishings. The cathedral was rebuilt in 1976 and is headquarters for the Russian Orthodox Church in Alaska.

Right - Humpback whales *(Megaptera novaeangliae)* feed at the surface of the ocean. Rather than teeth, plates of baleen, like a strainer, line the mouths of these giant mammals. They eat herring, other small school fish and tiny shrimp-like creatures called krill. Humpbacks use a variety of feeding techniques, including underwater exhalation of bubbles to concentrate prey (bubble netting), feeding in formation, herding of prey and lunge feeding.

Below - Ocean storm clouds filter the sunset over Sitka on Baranof Island. The town's residents work at the two colleges, in commercial fishing or fish processing and tourism. In its colorful history the town was a center for the Russian fur trade, American whaling and the site of a naval air station and U.S. Army base during World War II. Most recently it has served as a regional hub for logging and wood pulp processing.

Next page - Called "Sitka by the Sea," the town of 8,600 is located at the edge of sharp-peaked Baranof Island and is protected from the Pacific Ocean by the forested islands of Sitka Sound. The Russian-American Company moved its headquarters from Kodiak to Sitka in 1799, making Sitka the oldest non-Native settlement in Southeast Alaska. From its wooden stockade at New Archangel, Russian merchants and their Aleut slaves hunted sea otters for the lucrative fur trade, nearly wiping out the sea mammal. In the 1840s and 1850s, New Archangel grew prosperous and cosmopolitan and was known as the "Paris of the Pacific."

Previous page - Cannons on Castle Hill testify to Sitka's Russian heritage. Sitka residents celebrate Alaska Day every year with a ceremony on Castle Hill, the site where the transfer of Alaska from Russia to the United States took place on October 18, 1867. Russia sold Alaska earlier that year for $7.2 million, or about two cents an acre.

Left - Fishermen prepare their nets for their next trip to the fishing grounds. Commercial and charter boat fishing are important elements of Sitka's economy.

Below - The privately owned Rockwell Lighthouse was completed in 1985 by Sitka veterinarian Burgess Bauder who built it himself. Located on its own island, it is rented out as a lodge and is only 3/4 mile from downtown Sitka by skiff, which comes with the rental of the lighthouse. It is used by both boat skippers and airplane pilots as an aid to navigation.

Above - Juneau nestles at the base of Mount Juneau (3,819 feet) on the continental mainland. The view from Douglas Island encompasses Juneau's shoreline and visiting cruise ships.

Right - As seen from Mount Roberts, downtown Juneau fills the tide flats and the mountain flanks along Gastineau Channel. Founded in 1880 with the discovery of gold, Juneau's population is now approximately 30,000.

As the state capital, Juneau hosts the Legislature, which meets every year from January until May. The Capitol Building was built in 1931 as a federal building for the territorial government. Congress passed the Alaska statehood act in 1958, and Alaska joined the union as the 49th state in 1959.

The Governor's Mansion on Calhoun Avenue was built in 1912, the same year Alaska became a territory. Every holiday season, hundreds of lights decorate the exterior and the governor hosts an open house for the community.

Left - A parasailer glides down the steep slope of Mt. Roberts near Juneau with the Gastineau Channel and Douglas Island spread out before him.

Right - Float planes park in the airport float pond, near the Mendenhall Glacier. Floatplanes carry passengers, mail and freight to the towns and villages of the Inside Passage. They are also a practical way to reach the wilderness lakes and bays. Alaska has about 5,000 small planes, half of which are on floats at some time during the year.

Below - A fly fisherman casts at the base of a waterfall at Turner Lake, 18 miles southeast of Juneau. The U.S. Forest Service maintains a cabin here as well as 150 other locations in the Tongass National Forest which covers most of Southeast Alaska. The 16.8 million-acre temperate rainforest is home to dense growths of centuries-old Sitka spruce and western hemlock. It is the largest national forest in the United States.

Alaska Natives gather for Celebration, a gathering every two years in Juneau that draws Native Alaskans from around the state. The event is sponsored by the Sealaska Heritage Foundation. It features a week of song and dance in historic regalia, traditional foods, crafts and a parade.

A spruce tree carving by Tlingit carver Rick Beasley serves as a trail marker near the Mt. Roberts Tramway. The Haines area Tlingit Indians originally carved these markers on their trade routes to identify their territory and to make statements. These are the first known trail markers to be carved in this century and may be the only ones in existence.

Left - An eight-year-old holds a 35-pound king (chinook) salmon (Onchorynchus tshawytscha) caught in Juneau waters. The king salmon is Alaska's state fish. King salmon are the largest and least abundant of the five Pacific salmon species found in Alaska.

Middle - A proud youngster displays his Dolly Varden (Salvelinus malma) catch. The sea-run Dolly Varden ranges throughout Alaska's southern coastal areas. It spends the winter in lakes, migrates to the ocean at maturity in spring, and enters streams returning to lakes in the fall.

Below - A fisherman spin casts for salmon at Eagle Beach 28 miles north of Juneau, a favorite recreational spot surrounded by the Tongass National Forest.

The Red Dog Saloon boasts the charm and clutter of a frontier bar, with hunting trophies, life boat rings and sawdust on the floor.

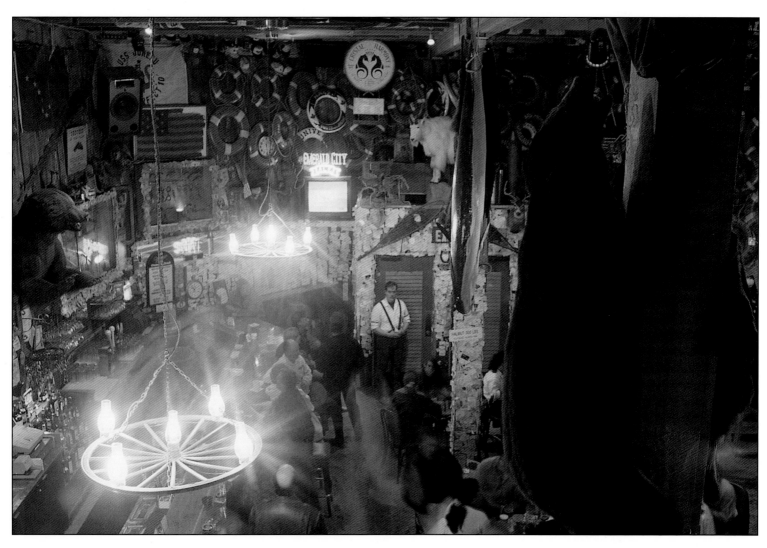

Above - A skater takes advantage of a cold, clear winter afternoon to enjoy the ice at Mendenhall Lake in front of Mendenhall Glacier.

Below - Skiers at Eaglecrest Ski Resort on Douglas Island near Juneau traverse to the East Bowls. Eaglecrest is owned by the city government and is a 20-minute drive from downtown Juneau.

Left - The Juneau Icefield consists of about 1,500 square miles of ice sprawling from Juneau east over the border to Canada and north almost to Skagway in Southeast Alaska. This Rhode Island-sized mass spawns more than 30 major glaciers including the Mendenhall, Herbert and Taku.

Below - Cross-country skiers track through the snows of Spaulding Meadows near Juneau. The capital city receives about 91 inches of precipitation, including 100 inches of snow each year.

Mendenhall Glacier

Left - Hikers on Thunder Mountain (2,900 ft.), about six miles from Juneau, pause to admire the Mendenhall Glacier that flows from the Juneau Icefield.

Below - With the Mendenhall Glacier as a backdrop, cross-country skiers head from Heintzleman Ridge to Thunder Mountain.

Next page - Golfers play at the Juneau Golf Course, built on the tidal flats of the Mendenhall River. Arctic lupine (Lupinus arcticus) and other wildflowers bloom along the fairway.

Above - The porch of the log skaters' cabin frames Mendenhall Lake and Glacier. For decades, this skaters' cabin has served as a warming hut for winter sports enthusiasts.

Below - A bicycler cruises the frozen Mendenhall Lake, which is 1.8 miles long. Some bicyclers make their trips safer in the winter by using studs on their tires.

Left - A helicopter flies tourists for a closer view of the Mendenhall Glacier. Juneau's glaciers are popular destinations for tourists. Floatplanes do fly-overs and helicopters land directly on the glacier or nearby mountain terrain, permitting visitors to explore the unique landscape on foot.

Below - An ice-hiking guide points out a crevasse to a young glacier hiker on the Mendenhall Glacier. Crevasses are created as the river of ice flows down over steep terrain.

Glacier Bay

Right - Campers pitch their tents along the forested shore of Scidmore Inlet. Eliza Scidmore was among the first tourists to visit Glacier Bay by steam ship in 1883, and wrote the first guide book to Southeast Alaska.

Middle - Kayakers paddle a safe distance from the face of Lamplugh Glacier in Glacier Bay National Park and Preserve, north of Juneau.

Below - Margerie Glacier empties into Tarr Inlet in Glacier Bay National Park and Preserve. The cliffs near the glacier host the largest black-legged kittiwake (Rissa tridactyla) colonies in the bay, averaging 2,600 nesting pairs. A black medial moraine snakes along one side of the glacier caused by rocks and other debris falling onto the moving glacier where it passes a rock outcrop.

Left - *Antique gas pumps are still functional at Gustavus's only gas station. Gustavus, a town of almost 400, is the gateway community for Glacier Bay National Park and Preserve.*

Below - *A cruise ship explores the ice-dotted waters of Tarr Inlet, near the terminus of the Margerie Glacier. The National Park Service limits the number of cruise ships to two per day in order to retain the wild character of the park's bays and fjords.*

Next page - *Boats anchored in Bartlett Cove, headquarters for Glacier Bay National Park and Preserve, enjoy vistas of the Fairweather Mountain Range. The nearest tidewater glaciers are approximately 43 miles up bay, accessible only by boat or float plane.*

Right - Two cruise ships advance towards the South Sawyer Glacier in Tracy Arm, part of the Fords Terror-Tracy Arm Wilderness Area 45 miles south of Juneau. Seals are commonly seen on the larger icebergs near the glacier's face. John Muir, founder of the Sierra Club, visited Tracy Arm in 1879.

Left - Pacific halibut (Hippoglossus stenolepis) cover the deck of a processing boat in Southeast Alaska. The delicate-flavored white fish is available year-round in Alaska restaurants and grocery stores.

Below - Fishermen haul in a halibut from the waters of Glacier Bay National Park and Preserve. Halibut are bottom-dwelling fish with both eyes on one side of their heads, the side that faces up when they are laying on the ocean floor.

Above - *The Tlingit Indians call Admiralty Island Kootznoowoo, "fortress of the bears." Admiralty Island has the largest concentration of brown bears (Ursus arctos) in the world, 1,600, or one per square mile.*

Center - *Sitka black-tailed deer (Odocoileus hemionus sitkensis) are native to the coastal rainforests of Southeast Alaska. On average their life span is 10 years. They feed on the leaves of shrubs in the summer and woody browse in the winter.*

Right - *Green's Creek Mine on Admiralty Island yields silver and other metals. Daily ferries transport workers from Juneau.*

Left - The Village of Elfin Cove is nestled on the north end of Chichagof Island, a refuge for fishermen from the fierce storms of Icy Strait and the Pacific Ocean.

Below - An Alaska Marine Highway ferry rounds a point on Chichagof Island, en route to the Tlingit village of Hoonah, population almost 900. Hoonah's ancestors originated in Glacier Bay, before the most recent advances of the Little Ice Age. Like most communities in Southeast Alaska, Hoonah is reached only by boat or plane.

Left - A Hoonah logger works on a log raft. Many of the Native regional and village corporations established by the 1971 Alaska Native Claims Settlement Act have turned to logging for income and jobs for their members.

Below - Giant booms lift spruce logs aboard a ship bound for Japan.

Left - Residents of the fishing village of Pelican transport their goods by sled in wintertime. Pelican, on Chichagof Island, does not allow cars on its boardwalk "road." Most houses and buildings are built on stilts at the water's edge.

Below - A state ferry docks at Tenakee Springs on Chichagof Island. Tenakee is another town, built at the ocean's edge, with a boardwalk for a road. Although some residents use motorized vehicles, none use cars. The town's mineral bath, Tenakee Hot Springs, is popular among retirees and Juneau residents who have summer homes there.

Left - *The proprietor of the Sea Wolf Gallery enjoys the spring sun on the porch of his log cabin studio and shop in Haines.*

Below - *The state ferry Columbia docks at Haines, where it discharges and picks up foot passengers and vehicles. Haines is linked by road to the Alaska Highway and is one of two northern Panhandle communities with road access to Canada's Yukon Territory and beyond to Interior Alaska.*

Right - Haines' small boat harbor contains many commercial fishing vessels. In the background the snow capped Chilkat Range rises to the west of the former U.S. Army Ft. William H. Seward, established in 1903 on 100 acres of land donated by the Presbyterian church when the U.S. and Canada were still negotiating the border between the two nations. Presbyterian missionaries gained influence at Haines in 1879 when the local Chilkat Tlingit Indians granted land on Portage Cove to the mission after a meeting with a church representative and his traveling companion naturalist and early Glacier Bay explorer John Muir. The town was named after a member of the church's mission board, Mrs. F. E. Haines.

Below - Leaves have begun to turn yellow on Haines' deciduous trees in the late summer. The town is to the right of Fort William H. Seward, later renamed Chilkoot Barracks to reduce confusion with the Prince William Sound community of Seward farther north. With close to 1,500 residents, Haines has begun to attract Alaskan retirees and is home to the Southeast Alaska State Fair in August. Nearby "Dalton City," was created by the Walt Disney Company as sets for the movie "White Fang" based on a Jack London novel. When the film was released in 1991, Haines residents had to travel elsewhere to see it because there is no movie theater in the town.

55

Skagway

Right - A resident walks the boardwalk just off Broadway, Skagway's main street. Skagway was one of two major staging points into the Yukon during the Klondike Gold Rush of 1896-1900. The other was Dyea, about nine miles from Skagway.

Below - A vintage vehicle of the Skagway Street Car Company gives tours of the town's historic buildings. The false front buildings on Broadway are part of the Klondike Gold Rush National Historical Park and retain the architecture of the gold rush days of 1897.

Left - *Buckwheat Donahue, a Skagway entertainer who recites the poetry of Robert Service and tells tall tales, poses among his town's famous flowers. Though windy, Skagway is much drier than its southern neighbors in the Alaska Panhandle.*

Below - *In winter, the snow blower engine clears snow from the tracks of the White Pass and Yukon Route Railroad. The engine is parked next to the National Park Headquarters for the Klondike Gold Rush National Historical Park in Skagway.*

Next page - *The town of Skagway nestles between mountains at the north end of Lynn Canal. Skagway ballooned to over 10,000 people in 1897 during the Klondike Gold Rush; today its year-round population is about 800.*

Left - The restored buildings on Skagway's Broadway serve thousands of tourists who visit every year, arriving mostly by tour ship.

Below - The Red Onion Saloon is a landmark in Skagway, once housing a brothel upstairs. At right is the gilded dome of the Golden North Hotel.

Next page - Flowers decorate the wooden boardwalk on Broadway in Skagway. The city has been officially proclaimed the "Garden City of Alaska."

Left - A passenger train of the White Pass and Yukon Route Railroad descends from the pass on its return trip to Skagway. The narrow gauge railroad has 110 miles of track. The train climbs from sea level to 2,885 feet in 21 miles, making it one of the steepest railroad grades in the world.

Right - The steam engine of the White Pass and Yukon Route Railroad pulls into Skagway. The railroad was completed in 1900 to carry gold seekers over the steep coastal mountains into the Yukon Territory. The railroad's northern terminus was just past the Whitehorse rapids. From there miners could float the Yukon River to the gold finds at Dawson City. For many years the railroad transported metal ore down from the Yukon Territory to the Skagway harbor; today it carries passengers to the mountain summit at White Pass.

Left - A hiker along the Chilkoot Trail heads for Happy Camp on the Canadian side of the historic trail, the first campground after climbing the 3,739-foot summit. Modern hikers take three to four days to carry their 40-pound packs over the 33-mile trail. In 1898, the Canadian government required gold seekers to bring 1,000 pounds of food and gear in order to enter the country. They instituted this rule to avoid famine among the thousands of men and women who flooded north in the Klondike Gold Rush.

Below - Hundreds of canvas and wood boats are among the debris abandoned by gold seekers as they carried their thousand pounds of gear across the Chilkoot Pass.